My Bilingual Picture Book

Moja dvojezična slikovnica

Sefa's most beautiful children's stories in one volume

Ulrich Renz • Barbara Brinkmann:

Sleep Tight, Little Wolf · Lijepo spavaj, mali vuče

For ages 2 and up

Cornelia Haas • Ulrich Renz:

My Most Beautiful Dream · Moj najljepši san

For ages 2 and up

Ulrich Renz • Marc Robitzky:

The Wild Swans · Divlji Labudovi

Based on a fairy tale by Hans Christian Andersen

For ages 5 and up

© 2024 by Sefa Verlag Kirsten Bödeker, Lübeck, Germany. www.sefa-verlag.de

Special thanks to Paul Bödeker, Freiburg, Germany

All rights reserved.

ISBN: 9783756304288

Read · Listen · Understand

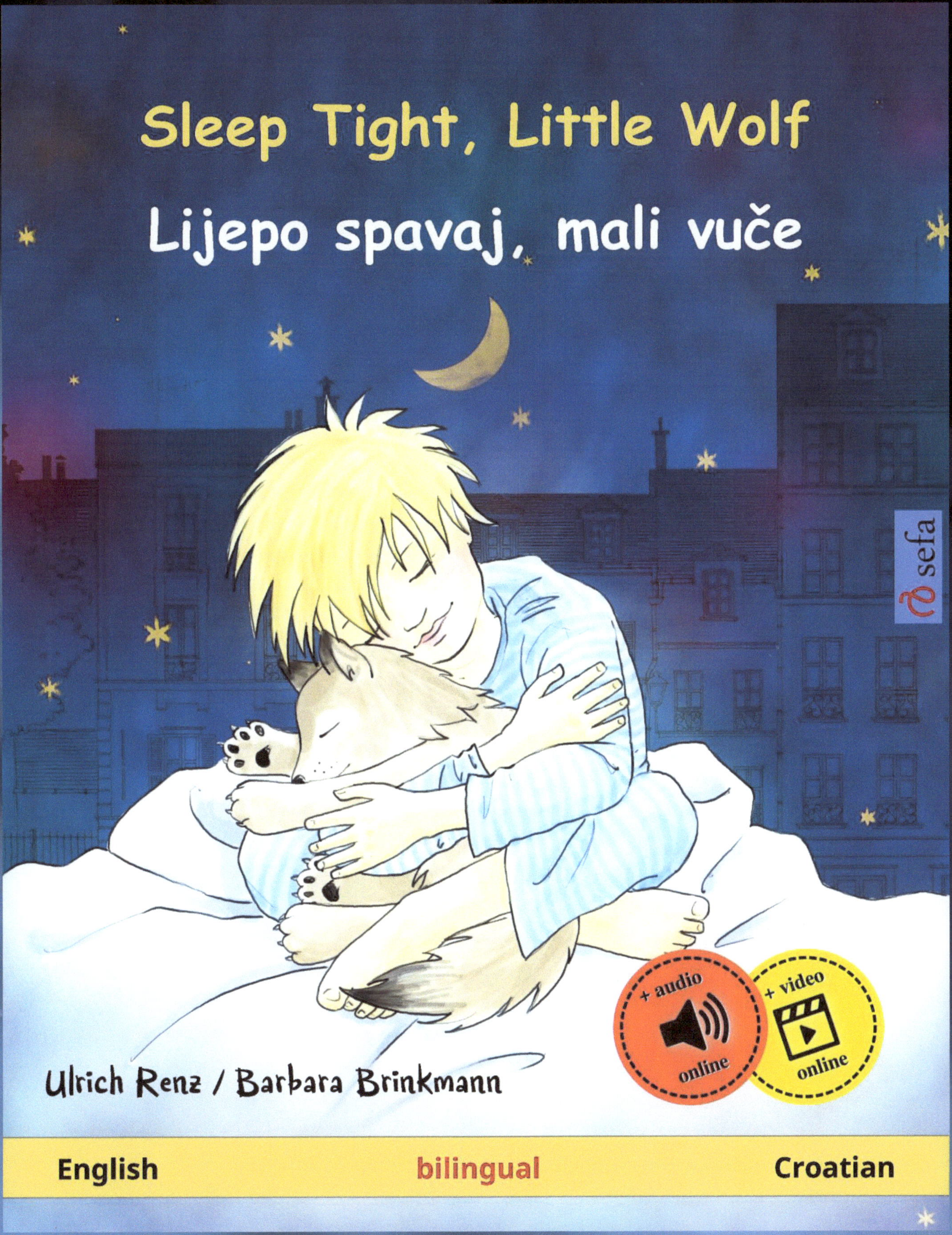
Sleep Tight, Little Wolf
Lijepo spavaj, mali vuče
sefa
+ audio online
+ video online
Ulrich Renz / Barbara Brinkmann
English
bilingual
Croatian

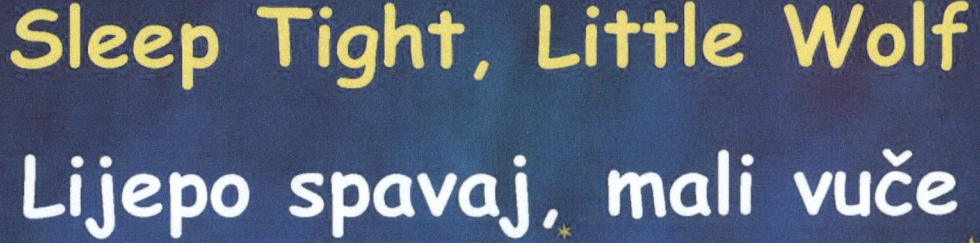

Translation:

Pete Savill (English)

Karmen Fedeli (Croatian)

Audiobook and video:

www.sefa-bilingual.com/bonus

Password for free access:

English: **LWEN1423**

Croatian: **LWHR1727**

Good night, Tim! We'll continue searching tomorrow.
Now sleep tight!

Laku noć, Tim! Sutra ćemo tražiti dalje.
A sada lijepo spavaj!

It is already dark outside.

Vani je već mrak.

What is Tim doing?

Što to Tim tamo radi?

He is leaving for the playground.

What is he looking for there?

Ide van, prema igralištu.

Što li tamo traži?

The little wolf!

He can't sleep without it.

Malog vuka!

Bez njega ne može spavati.

Who's this coming?

Tko li to sad dolazi?

Marie! She's looking for her ball.

Marija! Ona traži svoju loptu.

And what is Tobi looking for?

A što Tobi traži?

His digger.

Svog bagera.

And what is Nala looking for?

A što Nala traži?

Her doll.

Svoju lutku.

Don't the children have to go to bed?
The cat is rather surprised.

Zar ne moraju djeca ići u krevet?
Čudi se jako mačka.

Who's coming now?

Tko to sad dolazi?

Tim's mum and dad!
They can't sleep without their Tim.

Mama i tata od Tima!
Bez svog Tima ne mogu spavati.

More of them are coming! Marie's dad.
Tobi's grandpa. And Nala's mum.

I dolaze još više ljudi! Tata od Marije.
Tobijev djed. I Nalina mama.

Now hurry to bed everyone!

A sad brzo u krevet!

Good night, Tim!

Tomorrow we won't have to search any longer.

Laku noć, Tim!

Sutra više ne moramo tražiti.

Sleep tight, little wolf!

Lijepo spavaj, mali vuče!

Cornelia Haas • Ulrich Renz

My Most Beautiful Dream
Moj najljepši san

Translation:

Sefâ Jesse Konuk Agnew (English)

Karmen Fedeli (Croatian)

Audiobook and video:

www.sefa-bilingual.com/bonus

Password for free access:

English: **BDEN1423**

Croatian: **BDHR1727**

My
Most Beautiful Dream
Moj najljepši
san

Cornelia Haas · Ulrich Renz

English · bilingual · Croatian

Lulu can't fall asleep. Everyone else is dreaming already – the shark, the elephant, the little mouse, the dragon, the kangaroo, the knight, the monkey, the pilot. And the lion cub. Even the bear has trouble keeping his eyes open ...

Hey bear, will you take me along into your dream?

Lulu ne može da zaspi. Svi ostali već sanjaju—morski pas, slon, mali miš, zmaj, klokan, vitez, majmun, pilot. I lavić. Čak i medvjedu se gotovo zatvaraju oči...

Čuj Medo, jel me uzmeš sa sobom u tvoj san?

And with that, Lulu finds herself in bear dreamland. The bear catches fish in Lake Tagayumi. And Lulu wonders, who could be living up there in the trees?

When the dream is over, Lulu wants to go on another adventure. Come along, let's visit the shark! What could he be dreaming?

I već se Lulu nađe u medvjeđoj zemlji snova. Medvjed hvata ribe u Tagayumi jezeru. A Lulu se pita, tko li to tamo gore u stablu stanuje? Kada je san završen, Lulu želi doživjeti još više. Dođi, posjetimo morskog psa! O čemu li on sanja?

The shark plays tag with the fish. Finally he's got some friends! Nobody's afraid of his sharp teeth.

When the dream is over, Lulu wants to go on another adventure. Come along, let's visit the elephant! What could he be dreaming?

Morski pas se igra lovice sa ribama. Konačno ima prijatelje! Nitko se ne boji njegovih oštrih zuba.

Kada je san završen, Lulu želi doživjeti još više. Dođite, posjetimo slona! O čemu li on sanja?

The elephant is as light as a feather and can fly! He's about to land on the celestial meadow.

When the dream is over, Lulu wants to go on another adventure. Come along, let's visit the little mouse! What could she be dreaming?

Slon je lak kao jedno pero i može da leti! Uskoro će sletjeti na nebesku livadu.
Kada je san završen, Lulu želi doživjeti još više. Dođite, posjetimo malog miša! O čemu li on sanja?

The little mouse watches the fair. She likes the roller coaster best. When the dream is over, Lulu wants to go on another adventure. Come along, let's visit the dragon! What could she be dreaming?

Mali miš gleda zabavni park. Najviše mu se sviđa vijugava željeznica. Kada je san završen, Lulu želi doživjeti još više. Dođite, posjetimo zmaja! O čemu li on sanja?

The dragon is thirsty from spitting fire. She'd like to drink up the whole lemonade lake.

When the dream is over, Lulu wants to go on another adventure. Come along, let's visit the kangaroo! What could she be dreaming?

Zmaj je žedan od pljuvanja vatre. Najradije bi popio cijelo jezero limunade. Kada je san završen, Lulu želi doživjeti još više. Dođite, posjetimo klokana. O čemu li on sanja?

The kangaroo jumps around the candy factory and fills her pouch. Even more of the blue sweets! And more lollipops! And chocolate!

When the dream is over, Lulu wants to go on another adventure. Come along, let's visit the knight! What could he be dreaming?

Klokan skače kroz tvornicu slatkiša i puni si tobolac. Još više plavih bombona! I više lizalica! I čokolade!
Kada je san završen, Lulu želi doživjeti još više. Dođite, posjetimo viteza. O čemu li on sanja?

The knight is having a cake fight with his dream princess. Oops! The whipped cream cake has gone the wrong way!

When the dream is over, Lulu wants to go on another adventure. Come along, let's visit the monkey! What could he be dreaming?

Vitez vodi bitku tortama sa svojom princezom iz snova. Oh! Krem torta je promašila metu!
Kada je san završen, Lulu želi doživjeti još više. Dođite, posjetimo majmuna. O čemu li on sanja?

Snow has finally fallen in Monkeyland. The whole barrel of monkeys is beside itself and getting up to monkey business.

When the dream is over, Lulu wants to go on another adventure. Come along, let's visit the pilot! In which dream could he have landed?

Konačno da i jednom padne snijeg u zemlji majmuna! Cijelo majmunsko društvo se raduje i majmuniše naokolo.

Kada je san završen, Lulu želi doživjeti još više. Dođite, posjetimo pilota, u čijem li snu je on sletio?

The pilot flies on and on. To the ends of the earth, and even farther, right on up to the stars. No other pilot has ever managed that.

When the dream is over, everybody is very tired and doesn't feel like going on many adventures anymore. But they'd still like to visit the lion cub.

What could she be dreaming?

Pilot leti i leti. Do kraja svijeta, pa čak i dalje do zvijezda. Niti jedan drugi pilot nije to uspio.
Kada je san završen, svi su već jako umorni i ne žele više tako puno doživjeti. Ali lavića žele još posjetiti. O čemu li on sanja?

The lion cub is homesick and wants to go back to the warm, cozy bed.
And so do the others.

And thus begins ...

Lavić ima čežnju za domom i želi se vratiti u topli i udoban krevet.
I ostali isto tako.

I tamo počinje ...

... Lulu's
most beautiful dream.

... Lulin
najljepši san.

Ulrich Renz • Marc Robitzky

The Wild Swans

Divlji Labudovi

Translation:

Ludwig Blohm, Pete Savill (English)

Karmen Fedeli (Croatian)

Audiobook and video:

www.sefa-bilingual.com/bonus

Password for free access:

English: **WSEN1423**

Croatian: **WSHR1727**

Ulrich Renz · Marc Robitzky

The Wild Swans

Divlji Labudovi

Based on a fairy tale by

Hans Christian Andersen

English — bilingual — Croatian

Once upon a time there were twelve royal children – eleven brothers and one older sister, Elisa. They lived happily in a beautiful castle.

Jednom davno, živjelo je dvanaest kraljevske djece– jedanaest braće i jedna starija sestra, Elisa. Živjeli su sretno u prekrasnom dvorcu.

One day the mother died, and some time later the king married again. The new wife, however, was an evil witch. She turned the eleven princes into swans and sent them far away to a distant land beyond the large forest.

Jednog dana umrla je majka, a nešto kasnije se ponovno oženio. Međutim, nova žena bila je zla vještica. Sa čarolijom pretvorila je tih jedanaestero prinčeva u labudove i poslala ih je u jednu daleku zemlju izvan velike šume.

She dressed the girl in rags and smeared an ointment onto her face that turned her so ugly, that even her own father no longer recognized her and chased her out of the castle. Elisa ran into the dark forest.

Djevojku je oblačila u krpe i mazala joj lice sa ružnom masti, tako da ju čak i njezin otac nije više prepoznao i otjerao je iz dvorca. Elisa je pobjegla u mračnu šumu.

Now she was all alone, and longed for her missing brothers from the depths of her soul. As the evening came, she made herself a bed of moss under the trees.

Sada je bila sasvim sama i čeznula je za svojom nestalom braćom iz dubine svoje duše. Uvečer napravila si je krevet od mahovine ispod drveća.

The next morning she came to a calm lake and was shocked when she saw her reflection in it. But once she had washed, she was the most beautiful princess under the sun.

Sljedećeg jutra stigla je na jedno mirno jezero i uplašila se kad je vidjela svoj odraz u vodi. No, nakon što se oprala, bila je najljepše kraljevsko dijete pod suncem.

After many days Elisa reached the great sea. Eleven swan feathers were bobbing on the waves.

Nakon mnogo dana, Elisa je stigla do velikog mora. Na valovima ljuljalo se jedanaest labudovih pera.

As the sun set, there was a swooshing noise in the air and eleven wild swans landed on the water. Elisa immediately recognized her enchanted brothers. They spoke swan language and because of this she could not understand them.

Dok je sunce zalazilo, šum je bio u zraku i jedanaest divljih labudova sletjelo je na vodu. Elisa je odmah prepoznala svoju začaranu braću. Ali pošto su govorili labuđi jezik, nije ih mogla razumjeti.

During the day the swans flew away, and at night the siblings snuggled up together in a cave.

One night Elisa had a strange dream: Her mother told her how she could release her brothers from the spell. She should knit shirts from stinging nettles and throw one over each of the swans. Until then, however, she was not allowed to speak a word, or else her brothers would die.
Elisa set to work immediately. Although her hands were burning as if they were on fire, she carried on knitting tirelessly.

Danju labudovi su odlijetali, a noću sestra i braća su spavali priljubljeni jedan uz drugog u jednoj špilji.

Jedne noći, Elisa je sanjala čudan san: Majka joj je rekla kako bi mogla osloboditi svoju braću. Od koprive neka isplete za svakog labuda jednu košuljicu koju će im nabaciti. Ali do tada nije smjela govoriti niti riječ jer bi inače njena braća morala umrijeti.
Elisa je odmah počela raditi. Iako su joj ruke gorile poput vatre, neumorno je plela dalje.

One day hunting horns sounded in the distance. A prince came riding along with his entourage and he soon stood in front of her. As they looked into each other's eyes, they fell in love.

Jednog dana oglasili su se lovački rogovi u daljini. Jedan princ je dojahao na konju sa svojom pratnjom i već uskoro je stao pred njom. Kad su jedno drugome pogledali u oči, zaljubili su se.

The prince lifted Elisa onto his horse and rode to his castle with her.

Princ je podignuo Elisu na svog konja i odveo je u svoj dvorac.

The mighty treasurer was anything but pleased with the arrival of the silent beauty. His own daughter was meant to become the prince's bride.

Moćni čuvar kraljevskog blaga bio je sve samo ne zadovoljan sa dolaskom nijeme ljepotice. Njegova vlastita kći trebala je biti prinčeva nevjesta.

Elisa had not forgotten her brothers. Every evening she continued working on the shirts. One night she went out to the cemetery to gather fresh nettles. While doing so she was secretly watched by the treasurer.

Elisa nije zaboravila svoju braću. Svake večeri nastavila je plesti košulje. Jedne noći otišla je na groblje da ubere svježe koprive. Čuvar blaga ju je tajno promatrao.

As soon as the prince was away on a hunting trip, the treasurer had Elisa thrown into the dungeon. He claimed that she was a witch who met with other witches at night.

Čim je princ otišao u lov, čuvar blaga je dao baciti Elisu u tamnicu. Tvrdio je da je ona vještica koja se noću sastaje s drugim vješticama.

At dawn, Elisa was fetched by the guards. She was going to be burned to death at the marketplace.

U zoru, stražari su odveli Elisu. Trebala je biti spaljena na trgu.

No sooner had she arrived there, when suddenly eleven white swans came flying towards her. Elisa quickly threw a shirt over each of them. Shortly thereafter all her brothers stood before her in human form. Only the smallest, whose shirt had not been quite finished, still had a wing in place of one arm.

Čim je stigla tamo, iznenada doletjelo je jedanaest labudova. Elisa je brzo nabacila svakom labudu košuljicu od koprive. Ubrzo nakon toga, sva njena braća stajala su pred njom u ljudskom obliku. Samo najmanji, čija košulja nije sasvim bila završena, zadržao je jedno krilo umjesto ruke.

The siblings' joyous hugging and kissing hadn't yet finished as the prince returned. At last Elisa could explain everything to him. The prince had the evil treasurer thrown into the dungeon. And after that the wedding was celebrated for seven days.

And they all lived happily ever after.

Grljenje i ljubljenje braće i sestre nije imalo kraja kada se princ vratio. Napokon mu je Elisa mogla sve objasniti. Princ je zlog čuvara blaga dao baciti u tamnicu. A nakon toga, svadba se je slavila sedam dana.

I svi su živjeli sretno do kraja života.

Hans Christian Andersen

Hans Christian Andersen was born in the Danish city of Odense in 1805, and died in 1875 in Copenhagen. He gained world fame with his literary fairy-tales such as „The Little Mermaid", „The Emperor's New Clothes" and „The Ugly Duckling". The tale at hand, „The Wild Swans", was first published in 1838. It has been translated into more than one hundred languages and adapted for a wide range of media including theater, film and musical.

Barbara Brinkmann was born in Munich in 1969 and grew up in the foothills of the Bavarian Alps. She studied architecture in Munich and is currently a research associate in the Department of Architecture at the Technical University of Munich. She also works as a freelance graphic designer, illustrator, and author.

Cornelia Haas has been illustrating childrens' and adolescents' books since 2001. She was born near Augsburg, Germany, in 1972. She studied design at the Münster University of Applied Sciences and is currently a professor on the faculty of Münster University of Applied Sciences teaching illustration.

Marc Robitzky, born in 1973, studied at the Technical School of Art in Hamburg and the Academy of Visual Arts in Frankfurt. He works as a freelance illustrator and communication designer in Aschaffenburg (Germany).

Ulrich Renz was born in Stuttgart, Germany, in 1960. After studying French literature in Paris he graduated from medical school in Lübeck and worked as head of a scientific publishing company. He is now a writer of non-fiction books as well as children's fiction books.

Do you like drawing?

Here are the pictures from the story to color in:

www.sefa-bilingual.com/coloring